The Wild Side of Pet
Cats

Jo Waters

Raintree

www.raintreepublishers.co.uk
Visit our website to find out more information about **Raintree** books.

To order:
☎ Phone 44 (0) 1865 888112
 Send a fax to 44 (0) 1865 314091
💻 Visit the Raintree Bookshop at **www.raintreepublishers.co.uk** to browse our catalogue and order online.

First published in Great Britain by Raintree,
Halley Court, Jordan Hill, Oxford OX2 8EJ,
part of Harcourt Education.
Raintree is a registered trademark of Harcourt
Education Ltd.

Editorial: Melanie Copland and Saskia Besier
Design: Richard Parker and
Tinstar Design Ltd (www.tinstar.co.uk)
Picture Research: Maria Joannou and Alison Prior
Production: Duncan Gilbert

Originated by Ambassador Litho Ltd
Printed and bound in China by South China
Printing Company

The paper used to print this book comes from
sustainable resources.

ISBN 1 844 43479 6
08 07 06 05 04
10 9 8 7 6 5 4 3 2 1

**British Library Cataloguing in Publication
Data**
Waters, Jo
The Wild Side of Pet Cats
636.8
A full catalogue record for this book is available
from the British Library.

Acknowledgements
The publishers would like to thank the following
for permission to reproduce photographs: Bruce
Coleman Collection pp. **5** (R Meyer), **14** (Kim
Taylor), **16** (J Shaw), **21**, **23** (J Burton), **24** (J
McDonald), **4**, **10**; Corbis pp. **6** (T Brakefield),
12 (J Conrad), **15** (J Roberts) **25**; FLPA p. **22** (A
Visage); Getty Images p. **29** (Photodisc); Nature
Picture Library pp. **26** (R duToit), **28** (L Stone);
NHPA pp. **17** (Agence Nature), **20** (Kevin
Schafer); Oxford Scientific Films pp. **7** (E R
Degginger), **27** (H Schwind); Photographers
Direct p. **11** (Carmen Sisson); Tudor
Photography/Harcourt Education Ltd pp. **9**, **19**.

Cover photograph of a tabby cat, reproduced
with permission of NHPA (Rod Planck). Inset
cover photograph of a black panther reproduced
with permission of Nature Picture Library (Lynn
M. Stone).

The publishers would like to thank Michaela
Miller for her assistance in the preparation of this
book.

Every effort has been made to contact copyright
holders of any material reproduced in this book.
Any omissions will be rectified in subsequent
printings if notice is given to the publishers.

Contents

Any words appearing in bold, **like this**, are explained in the Glossary.

Was your pet once wild?

Did you know that your pet cat is closely related to wild animals? Finding out more about your pet cat's wild **ancestors** will help you to give it a better life.

There are many types of wild cat. The largest is the Siberian tiger. It can grow to over 3 metres and weighs as much as 225 kilograms. The smallest wild cat is the rusty spotted cat, which weighs about 1 kilogram!

Lions are one of the largest types of wild cat.

Popular pets

Cats can be kept in almost any home and they can be great companions. Although cats do not need walking like dogs, they do need plenty of space to exercise. They also need regular care and special food.

Cats are very popular pets. In the UK and USA, more people keep cats than dogs.

The African wildcat (top) looks very similar to a pet cat (bottom).

In the wild, cats have **adapted** to their **habitats**. When people talk about 'big cats', they usually mean lions, tigers, leopards, cheetahs and panthers.

There are also smaller types of wild cat. The cougar and the bobcat are smaller than lions and tigers. The Scottish wildcat is a little bigger and chunkier than a pet cat.

No spots
A panther is actually a type of leopard. Most leopards have spotty coats but panthers are black all over.

The clouded leopard's coat has large, cloud-like spots.

Pet cats are not the same as wild cats, although they look similar.

Coats and colours

Just like their wild relatives, pet cats have different coats. There are long-haired cats, like the Persian. There are short-haired cats, like the British shorthair. The Rex has short, soft, curly hair. Pet cats can also be many different colours, including black, tabby and '**seal point**'.

These Siamese kittens have seal point markings.

Where are cats from?

Wild cats live all over the world. Most big cats live where it is warm, but some, like the tiger, live in colder places like Siberia. Tigers also live in India and South-East Asia. Lions, cheetahs and leopards live in Africa. Bobcats and cougars live in North America and Canada. The African wildcat lives in the warm rainforests and woodlands around the **equator**.

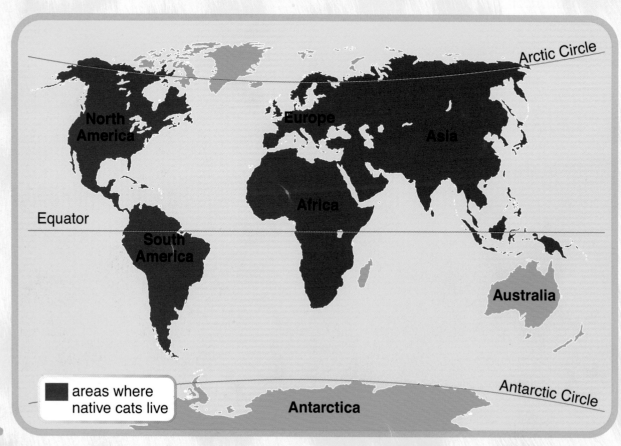

Arctic Circle

North America

Europe

Asia

Equator

Africa

South America

Australia

areas where native cats live

Antarctic Circle

Antarctica

This map shows that wild cats can be found in many places.

Allergies

Before you choose a pet cat, think about what type of cat will suit you best. Some people cannot keep cats because they are **allergic** to them. Is anyone in your family allergic to cats?

Remember that kittens need a lot of care and house training. Choose a kitten from a good breeder or from a family where you can see it with its mother.

This rescue cat needs a good home.

Rescue cats

You could adopt a cat from an animal rescue centre. There are many older cats as well as kittens that need homes. Older cats can be easier to look after than kittens.

Cat habitats

Wild cats make their homes in different places. Most cheetahs live on the open plains, where they can run and hunt **prey**. Panthers and tigers live in jungles and forests. They are very good at climbing trees.

Smaller cats like cougars can live in mountains, swamps, pine forests and even deserts.

Camouflage

A tiger's stripes help it to hide in long grass or amongst the leaves of a forest or jungle when it is hunting. They are a type of **camouflage**. *A leopard's spots do the same job.*

This leopard cub's spots help it to hide.

Pet habitats

A pet cat's **habitat** is its owner's home. Your cat still has the **instinct** to go out and hunt. Traffic and other animals can make this dangerous. Make sure your cat has a safe place to play in your house or garden.

Just like wild cats, tabby cats have stripes that help them to hide in long grass or trees.

All cats need somewhere to sleep or hide. A pet cat will have a bed somewhere in the house. You can buy special cat beds, but many cats choose their own sleeping place. This could be a warm shelf or a corner of a sofa.

Cat anatomy

Most cats have the same basic **anatomy** or body parts. Cats do not have a **collarbone** like humans. This allows them to be much more flexible than us.

Cats have very sharp teeth which they use for killing and eating **prey**. They crunch up bones and tear meat, but they do not really chew like we do.

Paws and claws

All cats have paws with soft pads and sharp claws. They use them for climbing, gripping and catching prey. They can draw their claws back into their paws when they are not using them.

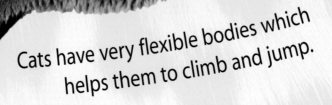

Cats have very flexible bodies which helps them to climb and jump.

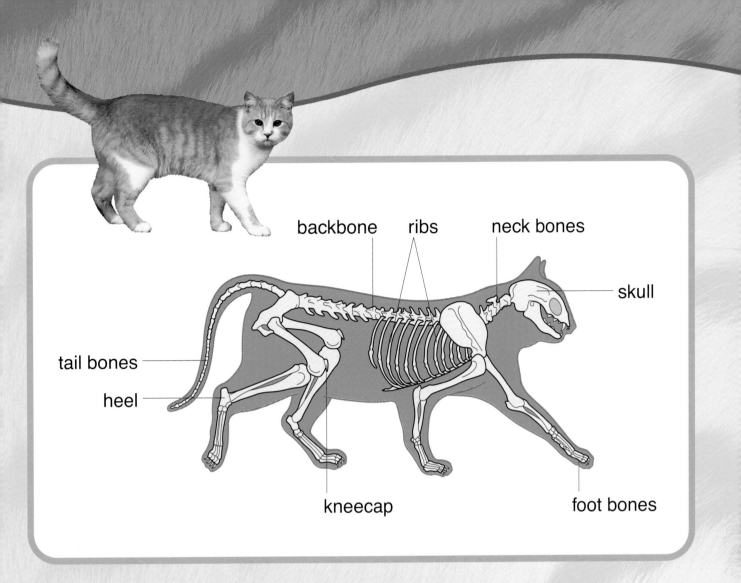

backbone   ribs   neck bones

skull

tail bones

heel

kneecap   foot bones

This drawing shows the skeleton of a cat.

In the wild, cats use trees to sharpen their claws. Pet cats also sharpen their claws. They will use furniture if they do not have anything else! It is a good idea to buy a scratching post for your cat.

Head first
Both wild cats and pet cats have special flexible ankle joints. This means that they can climb down trees head first!

Senses

In the wild, cats use their excellent senses to find food and stay out of danger.

Eyes and ears

A cat's eyes are set at the front of its head. This helps them to judge distances when they are leaping or hunting **prey**.

Cats' eyes are a different shape from ours and bulge out more. This lets in more light, so cats can see well in the dark.

Cats can move their ears in different directions to hear. They can hear more sounds than humans can, including the sounds made by small animals.

Pet cats also use smell and taste to choose what they want to eat. They have a special **organ** in the roof of their mouth. It lets them 'taste' smells. Cats can taste sour, salt and bitter foods. They do not really like sweet tastes.

Telling distances

Cats have **sensor** hairs all over their bodies. These long, single hairs tell a cat how close it is to things around it.

Cats can use their whiskers to judge space. If their whiskers can fit through a gap, the rest of the cat will fit as well!

Movement

Cats move by using **muscles** to work their legs. The back legs do most of the work when a cat is walking or running. The front legs are used for slowing down. Cheetahs can run at up to 96 kilometres (60 miles) per hour! They can only keep up this pace for short distances though. This means that cheetahs need to catch **prey** quickly or they go hungry.

Swimming

Most cats can swim but do not like to get wet. The Indian fishing cat is happy to hunt in the water.

Cats, like this cheetah, use their tails for balance.

16

Pet cats move in the same way as wild cats. A cat walking along a fence will **balance** itself just like a wild cat would.

Pet cats use stalking and pouncing movements like a wild cat would. You can see this when a cat is playing.

If a cat falls, it can usually turn itself upright and land on all four feet. This is called the righting **reflex**.

What do cats eat?

All wild cats are **carnivores**. They hunt and eat meat, and sometimes fish. Some wild cats occasionally eat grasses or leaves. Scientists think this is to help them get important **vitamins**.

Types of food

Lions hunt big animals like gazelles, zebras and antelopes. Tigers eat pigs, deer, antelopes and buffalo. Big cats need to eat a lot, but they do not usually need to eat every day.

The Indian fishing cat catches fish, frogs and snails from rivers and marshes. Tigers can catch fish too.

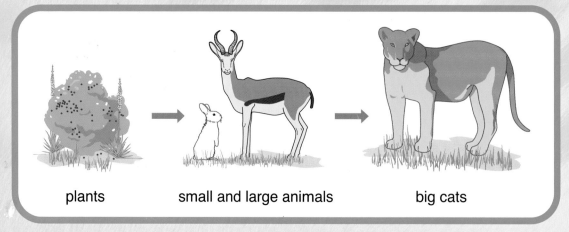

| plants | small and large animals | big cats |

This is how big cats fit into a **food chain**.

Make sure you know what to feed your pet cat and how much food it needs. Feed your cat two to three times a day. Follow the instructions on the packet.

Soft foods are made from fresh meat or fish. Dried cat foods are good for healthy teeth and some have added vitamins.

There are many different pet cat foods on sale.

Hunting

All wild cats have to hunt their **prey**. Lions and tigers stalk an animal and then pounce on it. The big cats are **camouflaged** behind grasses or leaves. They stalk their prey from **downwind** so it cannot smell or hear them coming.

Lionesses hunt in a group. Other cats, like cougars and jaguars, hunt alone.

The final bite!

Most cats kill small prey by biting the back of its neck. This breaks the animal's backbone.

Lions and lionesses kill big prey by hanging on to the animal's nose or or throat, so that it. it cannot breathe.

When a cat stalks and pounces on a toy, it is 'hunting' the toy, just like a wild cat hunts its prey.

Hunting at home

Pet cats still have hunting **instincts**. They may try to catch mice, rats or small birds. They may bring these to show you. They see you as part of their family, and they are trying to teach you how to hunt!

Fitting a bell to your cat's collar can stop it from catching birds. The bell frightens off the prey. It is a good idea to keep your cat inside until after it has been fed. A cat is less likely to hunt if it has just eaten.

Living in groups

Most big cats and other wild cats live alone. Wild cats mark the edges of their **territory** with urine to tell other cats to keep away.

Cats can **communicate** by sound. A lion's roar can be heard over 8 kilometres (5 miles) away! The cougar is sometimes called the 'mountain screamer' because of its loud calls.

Lion prides

Lions are the only cats to live in groups, called prides. A pride of lions usually has one male, and several females and young lions.

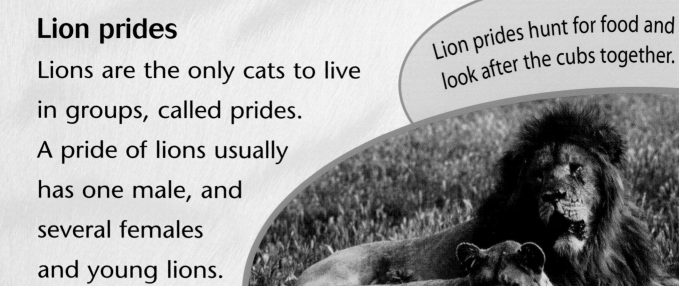

Lion prides hunt for food and look after the cubs together.

When two cats touch noses, they are smelling each other.

Most pet cats are friendly animals. However, if a cat has been alone since it was very young, it may not like being near other cats.

Cats make different miaowing sounds to ask for food or to be let outside. They purr when they are happy. They hiss or spit when they are angry or afraid.

Greetings

Cats that are friends will greet each other by touching noses. Your pet cat may greet you in the same way, weaving around your ankles or trying to jump up and touch your nose.

Sleeping

Most cats sleep a lot.
Lions can sleep for over
twenty hours every day.
After they have killed
and eaten, they can sleep
for a whole day without
doing anything else.

Many wild cats, like jaguars,
hunt at night or around dawn
and dusk.

Leopards and other wild cats can sleep in trees!

Sleeping places

Wild cats sleep wherever they feel safe. Lions sleep
in groups usually under the shelter of a tree or
rock. Snow leopards spend most of the day resting
on high rocks.

It is important for kittens to get lots of sleep because they grow while they are asleep.

Cats often take 'cat naps'. These are short sleeps during the day. The cat needs to have them to stay healthy and happy.

Pet cats sleep for about 16 hours a day. If your cat lives for 13 years, it will have spent over 8 years asleep!

Night hunters
Cats are often more awake at night because it is a natural time for them to hunt.

Every cat likes a quiet place where it can sleep without being disturbed.

Life cycle of a cat

Most big cats are **pregnant** for about 3 to 4 months. Most cats, like the snow leopard, only have two or three cubs.

In lion prides, all the cubs are born at around the same time. Then all the females share looking after them.

Lions and tigers can live for 15 to 20 years in the wild.

Young cats
Young big cats, such as lions and tigers, are called cubs. Young smaller cats are called kittens.

Young cats have a 'scruff **reflex**'. It makes them go limp so that their mother can pick them up and carry them in her mouth.

A pregnant pet cat will start to look fatter after about 6 weeks. Most cats give birth at around 9 weeks. A normal **litter** has between two and seven kittens.

Kittens do not open their eyes until they are 7 days old.

Kittens are born completely helpless. They start to walk after 2 to 3 weeks. By 10 to 12 weeks, they are ready to go to a new home.

Neutering

Cats can be **neutered** to stop them from having kittens. Kittens should be neutered when they are between 4 and 6 months old.

Common problems

Cats in the wild are **endangered** by damage to their **habitats**.

Some wild cats are hunted for their fur. The snow leopard has been hunted so much that it has nearly died out. Some cats are seen as pests and many are killed by farmers. This is a problem for the American bobcat.

Wild cats can also suffer from diseases and they may be hunted and killed by **predators** in the wild.

In danger!
The following types of cat are endangered:
- *tiger*
- *lion*
- *snow leopard*
- *Florida panther*
- *sand cat*
- *Geoffroy's cat*
- *jaguarundi.*

There are only a few hundred Siberian tigers left in the *wild*.

These are some common cat problems.

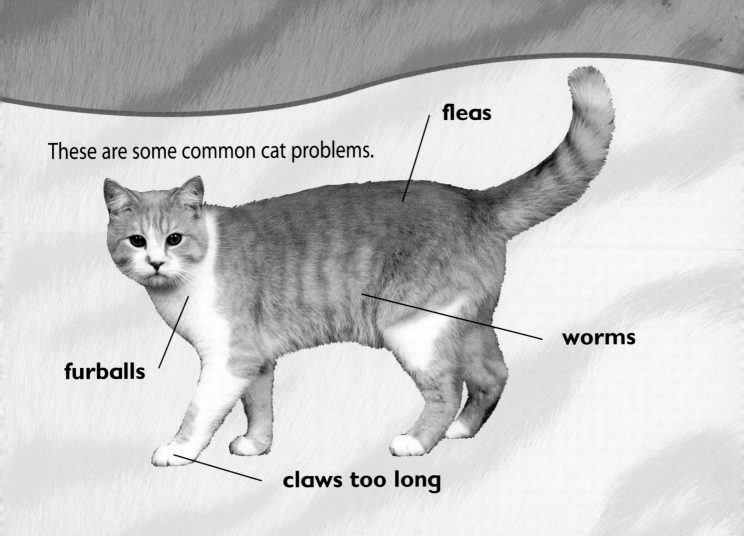

fleas

worms

furballs

claws too long

Pet cats can injure themselves if they fall or fight with other cats. Cats groom themselves by licking their fur. They swallow the loose hair. Fur balls form in the cat's stomach which they usually cough up. Grooming your cat often can help stop this problem.

Vaccinations

Cats need to be **vaccinated** to protect them against diseases. This happens when they are around 10 weeks old, before they are allowed outside.

Find out for yourself

A good owner will always want to learn more about keeping a pet cat. To find out more information about cats, you can look in other books and on the Internet.

Books to read

Cat Owner's Manual, Dr Bruce Fogle (Dorling Kindersley, 2003)

Pets: Cats, Michaela Miller (Heinemann Library/RSPCA, 1997)

Using the Internet

Explore the Internet to find out about cats. Websites can change, so if one of the links below no longer works, don't worry. Use a search engine, such as *www.yahooligans.com* or *www.internet4kids.com.* You could try searching with the keywords 'cat', 'pet' and 'wild cat'.

Websites

Cats Protection have a good site about looking after pet cats: *www.cats.org.uk*

Find out more about big cats at Big Cats Online: *dialspace.dial.pipex.com/agarman/bco*

Disclaimer
All the Internet addresses (URLs) given in this book were valid at the time of going to press. However, due to the dynamic nature of the Internet, some addresses may have changed, or sites may have ceased to exist since publication. While the author and publishers regret any inconvenience this may cause readers, no responsibility for any such changes can be accepted by either the author or the publishers.

Glossary

adapted become used to living in certain conditions

allergic react badly to something

anatomy how the body is made

ancestor animals in the past, from which today's animals are descended

balance the ability to stay upright

camouflage colour or pattern that lets an animal blend into the background

carnivores animals that only eat meat

collarbone bone joining the shoulder blade to the breast bone

communicate to make yourself understood

downwind away from where the wind is coming from

endangered in danger of dying out or being killed

equator imaginary line around the middle of the Earth

food chain links between different animals that feed on each other and on plants

habitat where an animal or plant lives

instinct natural behaviour which an animal is born with

litter kittens that are born to the same mother at the same time

muscle part of the body which contracts to produce movement

neutered animal that has had an operation so that it cannot have babies

organ part of the body that does a particular thing

predator animal that hunts and eats other animals

pregnant to have a baby growing inside

prey animal that is hunted and eaten by other animals

reflex automatic body reaction, done without thinking

seal point creamy body with dark brown or black ears, noses, feet and tip of the tail

sensor something that senses or feels things and sends a message to the brain

territory the area that an animal lives and hunts in

vaccinate an injection that protects an animal from disease

vitamin chemical that the body needs to stay healthy

Index

Titles in the *Wild Side of Pets* series include:

Hardback   1 844 43479 6

Hardback   1 844 43478 8

Hardback   1 844 43480 X

Hardback   1 844 43483 4

Hardback   1 844 43481 8

Hardback   1 844 43482 6

Find out about the other titles in this series on our website www.raintreepublishers.co.uk